# My Friends & Me
## Storybook

## Contents

**AGS**®

American Guidance Service
Circle Pines, Minnesota 55014-1796

A   10   9   8   7   6   5   4   3   2   1
ISBN 0-88671-326-9

D1466040

When Candoo and Willdoo first came to school, they were very excited and happy. They thought it would be wonderful to have so many other children to play with and so many things to do.

They looked around the classroom and hardly knew what to try first. Everything looked so interesting! Candoo decided that he would like to color. The crayons were all bright colors, and he liked the big sheets of paper. He'd have lots of room to draw a fine picture. Candoo sat down at a table where other children were coloring. But even before Candoo could find a crayon, a boy came over to him looking very angry.

"Hey," he said, "that's where I'm sitting." He pointed to the paper on the table in front of Candoo. "Can't you see my picture there? I just went to get another crayon."

Candoo hadn't meant to do anything wrong, and he felt bad. "I didn't know this was your place," he apologized. "At home I can sit in any chair I want."

"Well," the boy said, "at school, you have to take turns." He pointed to the table where the children were coloring, and Candoo saw that there were no empty places. "When one of us is done coloring, then you can sit in one of these chairs. You'll just have to wait your turn."

The boy was about to turn away and sit down in his chair when he saw the sad look on Candoo's face. The boy suddenly realized that Candoo really had not taken his chair on purpose, and he was sorry he had gotten so upset. He smiled at Candoo and said, "Why don't you go play with the blocks instead? There are only three kids over there, so there's room for someone else." That sounded like a good idea to Candoo. He smiled, happy that the boy wasn't angry anymore, and skipped across the room to the block corner.

Someone had built a beautiful high tower with the blocks. When Candoo saw it, he giggled happily. Then he took a deep breath, and pow—down went the blocks, all over the place!

A little girl, who had been getting more blocks from the shelf, turned around when she heard the crash. When she saw the pile of fallen blocks, she looked sad, as if she were going to cry. Another girl came over. Her eyes grew very large and round with surprise when she saw the jumbled blocks.

She looked at Candoo and shook her head. It was clear that she didn't like what she saw. "Ooooh," she said, "you shouldn't have done that! That was Maria's tower! Maria is the one who gets to knock it down."

"Yes," gulped Maria, who was now even closer to tears, "Josie's right. I get to knock down my own tower. You can knock down one if you build it yourself."

"Oh," said Candoo, "I didn't know about that. At home I can always knock down the blocks when I want to."

"Well, that's 'cause you're the only one building with them at home," said Josie. "At school lots of us are building, and we all get to knock down our own things!"

Candoo was really mixed up. Playing in school was certainly different from playing at home, and he was beginning to feel that school wasn't going to be as much fun as he'd hoped. He helped Maria build her tower again. Then he went over to talk to the teacher.

Several other children were with Ms. Carrigan. One of the boys was telling all about a lost dog he had found, and everyone was listening.

Candoo interrupted: "Ms. Carrigan, I wanted to color but all the seats were full, except one, and it belonged to a boy who just went to get another crayon to color his . . ." But Candoo didn't finish his sentence, because he suddenly noticed that no one was paying any attention to him! Not even Ms. Carrigan! She just went right on listening to the boy who was telling about the lost dog.

Candoo's eyes filled with tears. He felt like crying! Feeling very sorry for himself, he turned away. "At home Mother always listens to me," Candoo thought. Then he remembered what the boy with the crayons had told him about taking turns at the coloring table.

"Maybe talking is like that too," Candoo thought, and he felt a little bit more cheerful. "I'll bet I get a turn to talk when the boy is finished!" Now Candoo really felt better! So he went back to Ms. Carrigan and waited quietly till the boy finished telling the story.

When the boy was finished, Candoo said, "Ms. Carrigan, I think I'm going to like school. There are so many other children to play with, and so many things to do." Candoo felt happy when not only Ms. Carrigan, but also the other children, listened to him talk.

Then Candoo skipped over to the toy shelf. He found there were plenty of puzzles that no one was using, so he had a turn working with a puzzle.

Candoo thought about the things that had happened to him that morning. He had found out something very important: Playing in school with other children was not the same as playing at home alone. To help himself remember what he had discovered, Candoo made up this little verse:

When I'm playing in my home
All by myself,
I can play with any toy
On my shelf.

But when I'm playing at my school,
This is what I learn:
Share the toys with girls and boys.
Each one gets a turn.

# Candoo and the Big Slide

When Candoo started school, he was really happy to find a big slide! Candoo didn't have a slide at home, and sliding was one of his favorite things to do.

"Can I really slide every time I come to school?" he asked Ms. Carrigan eagerly.

"Yes, Candoo, you may," Ms. Carrigan said, smiling at him.

"Wow!" he exclaimed. "You mean, every day—every single day—I can go down the big slide?" Candoo almost jumped up and down, he was so excited!

Ms. Carrigan could see how happy Candoo felt, and she was glad. "Yes, Candoo," she said. "You may slide every day you come here. You really like to slide, don't you?"

"I lo-o-o-o-ve to slide!" Candoo called back to her as he ran over to the big slide.

Candoo climbed up the steps as fast as he could without falling off and sat down at the top. "Oh, boy, I'm really high up!" he shouted. "I'm as high as the sky. Maybe even higher! I'm a bird. No, I'm a cloud. Now I'm going down. Whee!" Candoo gave himself a push, and down he went.

At the bottom of the slide, Candoo wasted no time as he hurried around to the back and started up the ladder again. But on his way up the ladder, Candoo ran into trouble.

George was halfway up the ladder, and he was just standing there! He was not going up, and he was not coming down!

"Hey!" Candoo shouted. "Will you please get going? Come on, George, move! I want to slide!"

But George hung on tight and said, "I've changed my mind, Candoo. I'm scared! I don't think I want to go up after all. It's too high for me."

"Well, then," Candoo said impatiently, "get out of the way so I can go up."

"I can't," George said. "I'm afraid to climb up."

Candoo could see that George was really frightened, and he felt a little sorry for him. "Oh, well . . . okay, here . . . you'll have to back down then," Candoo said. He got off the ladder and, very slowly and carefully, George climbed down.

Candoo waited patiently until George finally got to the bottom of the ladder. But before Candoo could climb on again, Ellen jumped on the ladder and scampered up as fast as she could go. Then she sat down at the top of the slide. Candoo climbed the ladder and waited for Ellen to go down. But she didn't move. She just sat there! "Come on, Ellen," Candoo said. "Please go down the slide! Please!"

"I don't want to," Ellen answered. "I just like to sit here and look. I can see all over the room when I sit up here. I really like to look around."

Ellen sat there for quite a while, and Candoo began to yell, but it didn't do the least bit of good. When Ellen was finished looking around, she went down the slide. Then Candoo stopped yelling and happily sat down at the top of the slide, ready to slide again.

But when Candoo looked down, he saw Barry and Maria at the bottom of the slide with the big ball. Standing on her tiptoes, Maria put the ball as high up the slide as she could reach. Then she let it roll down. Barry tried it too, and then they both laughed.

"Please get out of my way," Candoo called to them. "I'm trying to slide." Candoo knew they might all get hurt if he went whizzing down while Barry and Maria were playing at the bottom of the slide.

Barry called, "Look, Candoo—this is fun! Watch the ball!" Barry rolled the ball down again. Maria looked up and smiled at Candoo, but Candoo didn't smile back. He didn't feel like smiling; he wasn't happy at all!

"Get out of my way!" he yelled as loud as he could. "I want to slide!" Barry and Maria both looked up at him in surprise.

Ms. Carrigan came hurrying over. "Candoo! Candoo! You sound very upset. What's the trouble?"

"Ms. Carrigan, I just want to slide," Candoo said. "You told me I could slide every time I came to school. But I've only gotten to slide once! First George wouldn't go up, and then Ellen wouldn't go down, and now Barry and Maria won't get out of the way! How am I supposed to slide? Would you please make them go away so I can slide?"

Ms. Carrigan was smiling. "You may slide, Candoo," she answered. "But Barry and Maria and Ellen may also use the slide. As long as we all play safely, we may use it the way we like. You and the other children will have to find a way to share the slide."

So that is what they did. While Ellen sat at the top and looked around, Barry and Maria rolled the ball down the slide. Then it was Candoo's turn to slide down.

# Ellen's Pets

In Candoo and Willdoo's classroom there were several different kinds of pets. There were some guppies, and there were even two white rats!

One day Ellen brought a pet to school. She brought it in a large box, a box so big that Ellen could hardly carry it. As she entered the classroom, Ellen was smiling her happiest smile.

Ms. Carrigan exclaimed, "My goodness, Ellen! That's a big box! Do you have something in there that you're going to show us?"

Ellen nodded eagerly, bobbing her head up and down. "Oh, yes," she said, "I have!" She felt so happy and excited about her surprise. "And my mama says we can even keep them here if you say it's all right, Ms. Carrigan."

Everyone was curious and wanted to know what was in the big box. Maria thought it might be something to eat, and Barry was sure it was something to play with. When all the children had gathered together and were sitting down, Ellen slowly lifted the lid off the box.

She reached inside and brought out two little blobs of fur. "These are guinea pigs," Ellen announced proudly. "My big sister has a pair of pet guinea pigs. And these are their babies. My sister said I could bring them to school. Ms. Carrigan, may we keep them here?"

"Well," Ms. Carrigan said, "we already have some pets to care for. And guinea pigs might require a lot of attention. What care do they need, Ellen?"

"My sister cleans the cage every day," Ellen said. "And she gives them fresh water and little pellets to eat." Ellen reached into the box again and brought out a handful of little hard, green things. "This is what we feed the guinea pigs," she said, and held out her hand so everyone could see the pellets.

"Please let us keep them, Ms. Carrigan!" the other children begged.

"I would have to be very sure that everyone was willing to help take care of these little animals," Ms. Carrigan said.

"I'll help!" said Candoo and Maria. Several other children said they would help too.

Ms. Carrigan smiled and said, "It seems we now have two new members in our group!"

"Hooray!" shouted the children.

"Weep! Weep!" squeaked the guinea pigs.

From the closet Ms. Carrigan took out an old cage that had once been the home of a hamster. Barry and Maria cleaned it out and washed it. Then Tina and George put in the food pellets and the water. When the cage was all ready, Lena and Candoo carefully put the two little animals into their new home.

The two guinea pigs ran around inside the cage making excited squeaky sounds. They nibbled a few pellets, drank a little water, and settled contentedly into a corner for a nap. Ellen said softly, "I can tell the guinea pigs like it here."

Every day when the children came to school, they took turns feeding their old pets, the guppies and the white rats. They took turns feeding the guinea pigs, too, and cleaning their cage. While two of the children worked on the cage, two other children played gently with the little animals and made sure they didn't get away.

One day it was Tina's turn to hold one of the guinea pigs while George and Kelly cleaned the cage.

The little guinea pig was restless, and Tina had a hard time holding it. "I know," Tina said, "I'll take my piggie for a ride in the doll carriage! It will enjoy the ride and settle down."

Candoo felt a little worried about that idea and asked, "Do you think it'll be safe in there, Tina?"

"Of course! I'll be very careful," said Tina.

Tina put the guinea pig into the doll carriage and covered it carefully with a blanket. She sang it a little song and rocked the doll carriage back and forth. "I'm putting the piggie to sleep the way Mommy does with our baby at home," Tina said.

"Weep, weep!" squeaked the guinea pig. Tina patted it gently and continued to rock the carriage. The guinea pig became quiet. "It's asleep," Tina whispered, feeling very pleased with herself. "I put it to sleep!"

Just then George called, "Tina, the cage is clean now. You can put your piggie back."

"In a minute," Tina said. "It's sleeping now."

George sat down to draw a picture. Tina wanted to watch him, but she was too far away to see what he was drawing. George looked as if he were enjoying himself, and Tina decided to go over and look at his picture up close. Suddenly Tina felt like drawing too, and she picked up a crayon and a piece of paper. She sat down across from George and drew a yellow circle on her paper. Tina was looking at her picture, trying to decide if she should add some more circles, when Ms. Carrigan announced that snacks were ready.

After everyone had eaten a snack, Ms. Carrigan read the children a story, and then it was time for music. Ms. Carrigan played a record, and the children marched and skipped and hopped around like bunnies. And then it was time to go home.

Just then Willdoo made an important discovery! There was only one guinea pig in the cage. "Oh, Ms. Carrigan, look!" Willdoo cried. "One of our little pets is gone! Where can it be?"

There was quite a lot of excitement after Willdoo's announcement that the guinea pig had disappeared. "Please," Ms. Carrigan said, "let's all be calm and try to think what could have happened to our guinea pig. I remember that everyone agreed to help care for the new pets, and I know you have done that. But somehow something has happened." Ms. Carrigan turned to George and Kelly. "Were both of the animals there when you cleaned the cage today?"

"Yes, they were," Kelly nodded. "And Tina and Candoo held them while we cleaned."

Candoo said, "I put my guinea pig right back. See—I had the white one, and there it is, right in the cage where it belongs."

"Tina," Ms. Carrigan asked, "did you put your guinea pig back in the cage too?"

Tina's hand flew to her mouth and she gasped.

"Oh, no! I for—for—for—got!" Tina stammered. "I forgot to put my piggie back in the cage! Now it's lost!"

Tina felt really upset. She was afraid that something *terrible* had happened to the guinea pig.

"Well," Ms. Carrigan said, "before we can go home, we'll all have to look for our little lost pet. Be careful not to step on it." The children started looking everywhere— under their chairs . . . in the cupboard . . . in the closet. As for Tina, she went straight to the doll carriage. She had pushed it into the corner when she went to see what George was drawing. She peeked under the blanket.

"Weep, weep?" squeaked her little friend. Tina smiled with relief. Gently, she lifted the little animal out of the doll carriage and carried it back to the cage. She whispered, "I'm sorry I forgot you, piggie."

The guinea pig made little happy squeaky sounds which told Tina that it was glad to be back in the safe, clean cage again, and Tina felt just as happy to see it there!

# Tina's Pictures

One day Ms. Carrigan told the children that she really liked the art projects they had been working on. She said, "You have all been making such nice paintings and drawings, and things made of clay and paper. I think it would be interesting if we had an art show, and then we could invite everyone to see your work. We can hang all your paintings and drawings up on the wall and put your other things on the tables. We'll ask your parents to come, and we can also invite your grandparents and aunts and uncles and brothers and sisters and some of your friends."

The children thought that was a very good idea, so everyone got busy arranging things for the show. They hung up everyone's artwork.

They hung Ellen's paintings near the door and put Candoo's picture of a friendly monster right next to Ellen's paintings. Willdoo's drawing of a house and George's design with blue lines were taped onto the chalkboard.

Khanh's picture of a ship, Tina's brown lines with red circles, and Tam's painting of bright yellow bananas were all on display. Pictures were placed all along the walls of the room.

When they were all finished, Ms. Carrigan looked around the room and smiled. "Oh, my," she said, "doesn't everything look lovely! I think we should hurry and write some notes to invite your families and friends to our art show."

The children made some invitations out of pretty paper. They decided what they wanted to say, and Ms. Carrigan helped them write the message. The notes read: "Please come tomorrow at eleven-thirty to see the artwork we have been doing at school." After school, each child took an invitation home.

The next day, the children's families and friends came to the art show. Mothers and fathers came. Willdoo and Candoo's grandma and grandpa came. There were big sisters, uncles and aunts, little brothers, and many friends.

In no time at all, the classroom was full of people who had come to see the artwork. They looked at the paintings on the walls and the clay models on the tables. They admired the drawings. They drank punch from small paper cups, ate cookies, and talked and laughed. Everyone seemed to be enjoying the art show.

When it was over, it was time for the children to gather their artwork and go home. All the artwork was taken down and stacked on Ms. Carrigan's desk. She handed the pictures to their owners, and the people began to leave.

Soon all the children, except for Candoo and Tam, had gotten their pictures and left with their families and friends. But Ms. Carrigan could not find Candoo's painting of the friendly monster or Tam's painting of the bright yellow bananas. Candoo and Tam and Ms. Carrigan all wondered where the pictures could be.

Ms. Carrigan frowned and said, "I don't understand it. Those pictures were here just a minute ago . . . I don't know where they could have gone." Candoo and Tam both looked as if they were about to cry. Ms. Carrigan felt sorry for them, because she could see how much they wanted to get their pictures back.

And that's when Ms. Carrigan noticed Tina standing near the door holding some large papers in her hand. Tina was watching Candoo, Tam, and Ms. Carrigan search for the pictures.

Ms. Carrigan told Tam and Candoo to wait for her while she walked over to talk with Tina. Ms. Carrigan could see that the papers Tina held were three big pictures.

"May I see your pictures, Tina?" Ms. Carrigan asked.

Tina held out the pictures. Ms. Carrigan saw that Tina not only had her own painting, but also Candoo's monster painting and Tam's painting of the bright yellow bananas.

"Tina," Ms. Carrigan said in a kind voice, "you have three paintings here. Are all of them yours?"

"No," Tina said, and her voice was very low. "But I want to take lots of paintings home." All of a sudden Tina wasn't feeling very well, and she didn't seem to be able to look at Ms. Carrigan.

Ms. Carrigan said gently, "But two of these pictures belong to Candoo and Tam because they made them, and they want to take their artwork home."

Tina did not look very happy, but after a minute she slowly walked over to Candoo and handed him his monster painting. Then she gave Tam's bright yellow banana picture back to him.

Candoo and Tam were happy to get their pictures back, and Tina realized that she was glad she had returned them. She was beginning to feel much better than she had felt a few minutes ago.

Ms. Carrigan smiled at Tina and said, "Tomorrow, when you come to school, you can draw some more pictures. And after school you can take all of them home."

Tina smiled up at Ms. Carrigan and said, "I'm glad I can make more pictures. Tomorrow I'm going to make *lots* more pictures. And I'll be able to take them all home because I'll have made them myself and they'll belong to me!"

# Willdoo Finds a Group

One morning Willdoo was feeling very bored. She wanted to find something interesting to do. She had spent part of the morning digging a hole. Now she was looking for something else to do, something different— but so far she hadn't thought of anything. Willdoo decided that she would shut her eyes very tight and then sit still and just listen. Sometimes listening helps a person find something to do.

Willdoo heard a bird chirping. She heard the sound of a car going by. Then there was the sound of children's voices. Willdoo's face brightened, and she opened her eyes. "Maybe those children are doing something I'd like to do," thought Willdoo. She decided to walk along the street and look for the children who were making the noise.

As she rounded the corner, she discovered that the sounds were coming from a group of children who were playing football. They looked as if they were really having a good time. The game looked exciting, so Willdoo felt that she wanted to play, too.

When she noticed that her friend Maggie was playing, she called to her. "Say, Maggie, can I play football with you?"

"Sure!" Maggie called back. "Come on over!"

"Willdoo is too little," somebody complained.

"No, she's not," replied Maggie. "Come on, Willdoo, you can play." Maggie showed Willdoo how to catch the ball and run with it.

Willdoo had watched Maggie carefully, and she thought she understood what to do.

But then, almost as soon as Willdoo joined the game, someone threw the ball right at her! She tried her best to catch it, but the ball was big and hard, and it came at her so fast that it knocked her down! The other children didn't even seem to notice that Willdoo was down on the ground or that she was hurt. Someone rushed by and picked up the ball after Willdoo missed it, and the children all went running back the other way. Willdoo was left alone, lying on the ground.

"Why on earth do they think this is fun?" she wondered. "It's too rough for me! Maybe I *am* too little for this game, after all. When I'm older, I'll probably like it better and want to play, but I don't like it now."

Soon Willdoo was feeling all right. She sat up and looked around for a minute. Then she decided it was time to find something else to do! She got to her feet and started walking again.

Janie and Jamie were in their backyard, playing in their playpen. Their mother was working nearby, raking leaves. "Mrs. Ross," Willdoo asked, "may I play with Janie and Jamie, please?"

"Yes, of course you may," replied Mrs. Ross.

Willdoo went over to the playpen. "Hi, Janie!" Willdoo smiled. Willdoo picked up a ball that had rolled out of the playpen and handed it to Janie.

"Goo," said Janie with a big, wet smile. The ball was a little too big for Janie to hold, and she dropped it. Sadly, she watched it roll away again. Willdoo picked up the ball again and put it down in the playpen. Janie gave Willdoo another big, wet smile.

Willdoo turned to the other baby. "Here, Jamie, want your toy?" She handed Jamie some jar rings attached to a string. The baby shook the rings and listened to them rattle. Then he dropped the rings and just sat staring at Willdoo.

At that moment, the ball rolled out of the playpen again, and Janie looked up at Willdoo, waiting for her to pick it up again.

Willdoo laughed. As she bent to pick up the ball again, she thought to herself, "Janie and Jamie are cute. But they don't know how to play the games I like to play. I guess I'm too old for them, and I'm too *young* to play with Maggie and her group." Willdoo said goodbye to the babies and walked on to see what else she could find to do.

Willdoo walked into the kitchen of her own house. The kitchen smelled good. Grandma was there, and she was stirring something in a bowl. Willdoo's father and her big sister were there too.

"Oh, Willdoo, I'm so glad you're here!" said Grandma. "We need help with the baking. All these cookies have to be ready to take with us to the picnic this afternoon."

"Goody!" said Willdoo. "I've been looking everywhere for a group to do something with. I tried playing with Maggie, but her group was too rough for me. I tried Janie and Jamie, but they don't know how to play with other children yet."

Grandma smiled at Willdoo and said, "Well, you are welcome to join *this* group. Wash your hands. There's a lot for you to do here."

Willdoo hurried to the sink and washed her hands.

"Now I've found a good group for me," she thought, as she climbed up on her stool to make cookies. "I'm doing something I like to do. Grandma needs help. She wants me to work with the others. Together, all of us will make a group—a group that I like!"

# Somebody's Job

The children have a playhouse on a vacant lot near Candoo and Willdoo's home. There are trees and bushes separating the lot and playhouse from the houses next door. The children are proud of their playhouse because they worked hard to build it. They think it's a wonderful place to play, and they really have a good time there.

One afternoon after school, as Candoo, Willdoo, and Barry were walking over to the playhouse to play, they suddenly noticed how much trash was lying around the lot. There were old, rusty cans in the grass by the trees; pieces of paper and bits of candy wrappers were scattered around too. There were even scraps of board that had been left over when they had built their playhouse. The lot really looked messy.

Barry stopped and stared at the playhouse. "Our playhouse is nice," he said to the others, "but look at that junk all around it. Look at those old cans—and the paper."

"It sure is messy," Willdoo agreed. "I guess people throw stuff here because no one lives here. But they shouldn't do that. I don't like to have it look like this around our playhouse."

"It's awful," Barry said. "I wish somebody would come along and clean it up."

Willdoo thought about that for a while, and then she said, "I have an idea. Why should we wait for someone else to clean it up? Why don't we do it ourselves? We could pick up all this stuff and put it in the trash."

"But why should we pick it up?" asked Barry. "That wouldn't be fair. We didn't throw all this junk around here and make this mess. The people who put it here are the ones who ought to clean it up."

"Some of this stuff has been here a long time," said Candoo, as he kicked a rusty can. "I don't think the people who dropped it here are going to come back to pick it up. But it must be somebody's job to keep the neighborhood clean."

"Well," Willdoo said thoughtfully, "we're the ones who play here. If we want it to look nice, maybe we'll have to clean it up."

Candoo looked around the cluttered lot for a moment; then he nodded his head and said, "I think that's a good idea, Willdoo. We could collect all this stuff and put it in a bag. Then we could put it in our trash can."

The children decided that maybe it was their responsibility to clean up the lot, so Candoo went home and asked for a trash bag. He brought it back to the vacant lot and the children began to fill it with the rubbish.

First they picked up the cans that were under the trees, and then they gathered up the paper around the lot. Soon the only things left were the pieces of board.

"I don't think we should throw all these good boards away," said Willdoo. "We might want to build something with them sometime."

"That's right," Barry agreed. "But at least we can put them in a pile, so they won't look so bad."

And that's what they did. They picked up all the wood scraps and stacked them in a neat pile beside the playhouse.

When they were all finished, they looked around at the lot. They liked what they saw, and they smiled at one another. They had worked together to clean up the lot, and they felt very proud of themselves.

# The Friendly Monster's Party

Candoo and the friendly monster were in the monster's pumpkin patch. "I have so many pumpkins I couldn't possibly eat them all," the monster said. The monster was quiet for a moment, and then it smiled. "I know what I'll do!" it exclaimed. "I'm going to make a lot of pumpkin pies, and then I'll have a party and invite my friends to eat pumpkin pies with me!"

"That would be a very kind thing to do, Monster," Candoo said. "Can I help you get ready for the party?"

"It's very kind of you to offer to help me, Candoo," the monster replied. "You can help me make the pies. Oh, my! Isn't this exciting? Won't everyone love coming for blue pumpkin pie!"

Candoo thought about that for a minute. "I don't know, Monster," he said doubtfully. "I'm not so sure Homer will love it. He doesn't like blue, you know. Hmm . . . I wonder if there's anyone else who doesn't like blue."

"Well, just in case there is," the monster replied, "we'd better get busy and make some red pies and some purple pies, too."

"Do you know what else we need for your party?" asked Candoo. "You! To sing a song for us! Everyone loves to hear you sing!"

It made the monster happy to hear Candoo say that. "How very kind of you to tell me that, Candoo! I'd love to sing at a party! I think I'd better get busy and practice. La-la-laaa . . . "

While the monster was practicing the song it was going to sing, Candoo began preparing the pies. As Candoo worked, he listened to the monster singing in its deep, deep voice.

"I'll surprise the monster," Candoo thought. "By the time the monster is finished practicing, I'll have the pies all ready. Let me see, now: I'll make three blue ones—the monster can eat those all by itself. And I'll make some purple ones and a red one. When they're done, I'll put them here on the table."

In a little while, the monster called to Candoo excitedly. "Candoo, Candoo!" the monster exclaimed, "I've practiced the whole song. Would you like to hear it?"

The monster rushed into the kitchen, ready to sing for Candoo. When it saw the table full of pies, it stopped, its enormous eyes opening even wider with surprise. "Oh, my!" the monster said. "What have you been doing?"

"I fixed the pies for the party," Candoo said. "Do you like them?"

"Oh, Candoo!" said the monster. "How kind of you! Those pies are beautiful! What a great surprise! Now the *song* is ready and the *pies* are ready, too. We can begin our party!"

The first guest to arrive was the big elephant. She liked pumpkin pie—any color. Candoo found her a great big chair to sit on.

"How kind of you, Candoo, to get a special chair for the elephant," the friendly monster said. "I guess you know that elephants can't sit on just any old chair. Look! Here comes Teeny, my little spider friend. She's so little—I'm afraid someone might step on her by accident. And how is she going to be able to see what's happening at the party from down there?"

"That's easy," said Candoo. "I'll find a high stool for her, so that she will be able to see over everybody's head."

Candoo found just the right chair for each guest at the party. He even got a nice green chair for Willdoo. And he made room for Homer the snake on the floor. Homer preferred being on the floor. He didn't care much for chairs.

After everyone had arrived, the monster stood up to speak: "By special request . . . I have been invited . . . uh . . . I have been told that . . . uh . . . I understand that you would like . . . uh . . . Would you like to hear me sing a song?"

All the guests shouted and clapped. "Yes! Please do! Sing us a song!"

"You really are kind, you really are," murmured the monster, feeling very pleased and flattered as it made its way to the piano.

This was the monster's song.
*(Play recording of Song 9, "I Did It and I'm Glad.")*

> I thought of something I could do,
> That would make you happy, too.
> Then I did it and I'm glad I did,
> Then I did it and I'm glad.
>
> I thought of something I could say,
> That would brighten up your day.
> Then I said it and I'm glad I did,
> Then I said it and I'm glad.
>
> When I see you're happy,
> Then I feel happy, too.
> When I see you smile,
> I feel like smiling, too.
>
> I thought of something I could share,
> Just to let you know I care.
> Then I did it and I'm glad I did,
> Then I did it and I'm glad.

When the monster finished its song, everyone stood up, applauding and cheering. "How kind of you to sing for us," the guests said.

The friendly monster bowed. It felt very proud that everyone had enjoyed the song so much.

"I've sung my song, and now it's pumpkin-pie time!" the monster exclaimed. "Candoo has made us all these pies. Help yourselves. Eat all you want! There's a choice of colors, so choose the kind you like best."

Willdoo had a piece of blue pie, and so did Candoo.

"I prefer red," squeaked Teeny the spider. She started eating her piece of pie. Suddenly she stopped and looked around the room. "Say! Where's Homer? Has anyone seen him? Homer, where are you?"

"Down here—I'm under the piano!" called Homer. "I'm stuck. I can't get out!"

"Oh, dear," said the monster. "We have to get Homer out of there! We have to raise the piano!"

The elephant came lumbering over, her trunk swaying as she moved. "I'll do it," she said, and she easily lifted the heavy piano.

Homer wriggled out from under the piano. "Thanks!" he said to the big elephant. "I'm glad to be out of there!"

"Homer," the friendly monster said, "Candoo made some red and purple pies especially for you because he knew you didn't like blue."

"He did?" Homer smiled. "How kind and thoughtful that was! Thank you, Candoo!"

"You're welcome," Candoo replied. "I enjoyed doing it."

Everyone finished the pie, and soon the party was over. It was time to go home.

"Thank you for inviting us over to your house," the guests said. "Thank you for singing your song. And thank you for being so kind!"

"Oh, my," said the monster, blushing a bright red. It felt embarrassed by all the praise. "Thank you for coming!"

# Tina Can't

When Tina started coming to Candoo's school, she was
so little that everyone wanted to help her. The children
showed her where things in the classroom were and
what to do. For a while, all the children enjoyed helping
Tina. But as the days went by, it seemed to the children
that it was time for Tina to begin to do some things for
herself.

But Tina still came to school in the mornings and stood by the door until someone noticed her and said, "Tina, hang up your coat and come play."

Tina would always answer, "You do it. Tina can't."

At singing time, Tina would stay where she was until someone called to her, "Come on, Tina, don't you want to sing?"

But by then, Tina had missed the first few songs.

When everyone went outside to play, Tina waited and waited for someone to tell her to come too. By the time she joined the group, all the tricycles were always taken, so Tina never got a turn to ride.

During playtime one morning, Candoo noticed Tina standing in a corner, waiting for someone to help her.

"Tina," Candoo asked, "why don't you get something to play with?"

"I can't," Tina replied. "I don't know how. You do it for me."

"You *can* do it," said Candoo. "Look at all the toys on the shelf. Which one would you like to play with?"

Tina smiled and said, "The beads!"

"Okay," said Candoo. "You just walk right over there and get the beads."

"No," said Tina. "You do it for me. I might spill the beads."

"That's all right, Tina," said Candoo. "If you spill them, you can just pick them up again."

Tina thought about that and decided to take Candoo's advice. She walked over to the shelf, took down the beads, and started playing with them. Candoo played with a puzzle.

When playtime was over, the children put away their toys and gathered for a treat. They were going to share Maria's birthday cake.

Candoo had put away his puzzle and was about to join the others, when he realized that Tina was still sitting on the floor playing with the beads. "Hurry up, Tina," Candoo said. "Put your beads away now. We're going to have some cake and ice cream."

"I can't do it, Candoo," Tina complained. "You put them away for me."

"Oh, no," said Candoo. "You have to put the beads away because *you* were playing with them. That's only fair." Candoo felt annoyed with Tina, and he wondered if she would ever learn to do things for herself.

Candoo went over to join the rest of the group. Ms. Carrigan and the children were singing "Happy Birthday" to Maria.

Tina sat on the floor for a long time, looking at the children and then at the beads. Finally, she picked up the beads, put them back in the box, and placed the box on the toy shelf.

Tina went over to Ms. Carrigan, who was standing at the table where the children were eating their cake. "Ms. Carrigan," Tina said, "I put the beads away. And I did it all by myself! Nobody had to help me." Tina was proud. "May I have some cake too?" she asked.

"We were wondering where you were, Tina," Ms. Carrigan replied. "I'm glad to hear that you put away the beads all by yourself. There are many things we do need help with, because they are hard for us to do by ourselves. But there are other things we can do quite well alone. It makes me feel happy to see you doing those things you can manage by yourself."

# Candoo Gets Help

When Candoo arrived at his classroom one morning, he did not see anyone in the room. The door was unlocked, but the room was dark.

"Ms. Carrigan will come in a minute," Candoo thought. "The first thing I have to do is turn on a light in here."

Candoo went over to the light switch and reached up to turn it on. He stretched and stretched, but it was too high for him to reach.

"I guess turning on the lights is one of the things that grown-ups can do more easily than children," he said to himself. "But I can do it if I have to."

Candoo pulled a little chair over to the light switch. He climbed up on the chair and turned on the lights in the room.

"That's better," said Candoo, as he put the chair back where he found it. "Now . . . I have the whole classroom to myself." He looked around the room. "What will I do?"

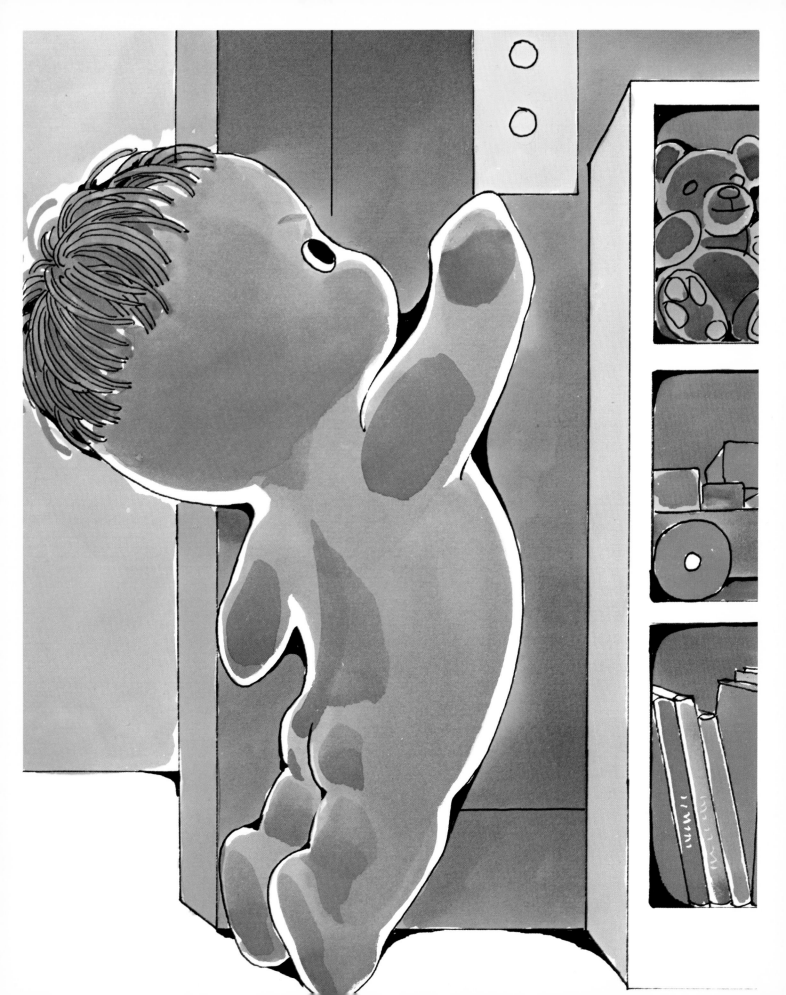

One of Candoo's favorite things to do in school was to listen to Ms. Carrigan read a story, so Candoo went over and sat down on the rug. That was where he always sat when Ms. Carrigan read to the children. But even though he sat very still, he did not hear a story— because there was no story to hear. There was no Ms. Carrigan to read it. Candoo could look at the pictures in the storybook, but he couldn't hear the words until someone came who could read them.

Candoo got up and went to the kitchen. "My next most favorite thing at school is having cookies and juice," he thought. "Maybe I will do that."

But when Candoo looked in the kitchen, he saw that the juice had not been made yet. The jar with the orange-colored powder in it was on the counter. Candoo smiled. He'd make the juice and surprise the teacher. She'd be so pleased.

But Candoo couldn't remember how much powder to use. And he wasn't sure how much water to add. Then, when he turned on the faucet, water splashed all over, getting Candoo wet.

When Candoo thought he had the mixture the way Ms. Carrigan would have made it—the color looked just about right—he put a spoonful in his mouth, and made an awful face. "Maybe it *looks* like orange juice," he said, "but it sure doesn't *taste* like orange juice. Ugh! It's terrible!"

Candoo decided to leave the juice on the counter for Ms. Carrigan. He was sure she would be able to help. He knew she would make the juice taste just right. "Children can make the juice sometimes if there's a grown-up to help," he said to himself. "But, most of the time, fixing food is something grown-ups do for us."

Since the juice wasn't ready, Candoo went over to the play kitchen and pretended to bake cookies. He sat down at the table and imagined he was eating. His make-believe cookies were delicious, but Candoo was beginning to feel a little lonesome. Where was everyone? He wished that someone else would come.

Sighing, he went over to the block corner and sat down on the floor to build something with the blocks. "Blocks," he thought, "are one thing I can do all by myself."

Just then, Ms. Carrigan came in. When she saw Candoo, she smiled and said, "Well, look who came in first today. Good morning, Candoo." Candoo felt very happy to see his teacher. He told her about the orange juice he had tried to make, and they went into the kitchen together. Ms. Carrigan added a little more water to the container, and to Candoo's great surprise, the juice tasted just fine.

In a little while, the rest of the children arrived, and the day at school began.

# The Lost Visitor

When the children came to school one morning, Ms. Carrigan said she had a surprise for them. They had a visitor. "This visitor is different from the ones we usually have. She cannot sit beside you at the table, because she doesn't have any legs. She cannot take turns with you when it's time to wash your hands, because she doesn't have any hands. And she won't sing songs with us or tell us a story, because she doesn't have a voice!"

"Who could it be? What could it be?" asked the children.

"It's not a person," George said, "because a person could sit with us."

"You're right, George," Ms. Carrigan said. "It's not a person."

"Is it an animal?" someone wanted to know.

"What animal doesn't have a voice?" Tina asked.

"Hmm, I can't think of one," said George, frowning. "Maybe it's not an animal, after all."

After the children had all taken turns guessing, Ms. Carrigan smiled and said, "I think it's time for you to meet our visitor."

Ms. Carrigan lifted the blanket off the big box next to her. The children could see that the box was made of glass. It looked like a tank for fish. The children looked inside. Ms. Carrigan looked inside.

"Ms. Carrigan," José asked, "is our visitor invisible? I can't see her."

Candoo peered into the box. "Is she something very tiny swimming in that pan of water?" he asked. The pan of water was the only thing in the glass box.

Ms. Carrigan looked very surprised. "Oh, dear! What has happened to our visitor? She was in the box when I covered it up. I don't know where she could be!" Ms. Carrigan wasn't laughing anymore. She looked upset. "This morning, before you came, I put the blanket over the tank so I could surprise you, and she must have gotten out somehow!"

"What was it? What was in there?" the children wanted to know.

Ms. Carrigan said, "Our visitor is a snake—a boa constrictor.

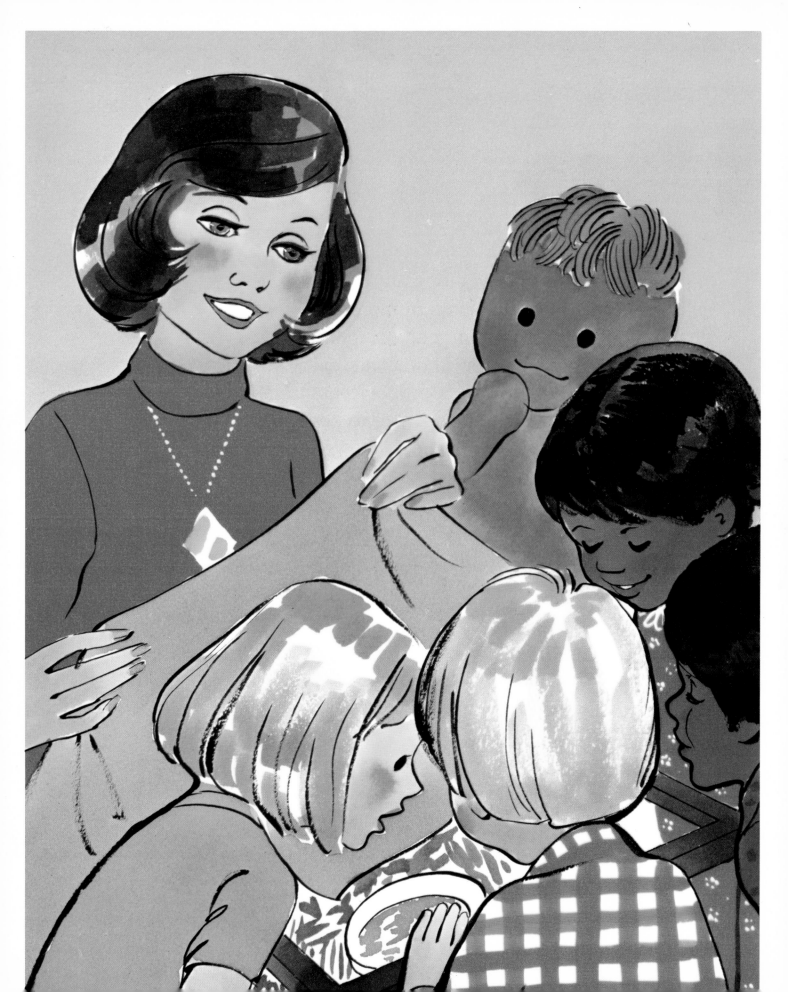

"Now, I know not everybody likes snakes," Ms. Carrigan said. She could see that some of the children felt uneasy about the thought of a snake loose in the classroom, and she wanted to reassure everyone. "This snake will not hurt you," Ms. Carrigan told the children. "I would not bring a dangerous snake to school. But we do have to find her! Let's start looking in all the hiding places we can think of!"

The children began searching the classroom for the missing snake. They looked everywhere! They looked on the toy shelves and in the dollhouse. They looked under the sink and in the block corner.

"Maybe she didn't go very far," said Candoo thoughtfully, as he tried to figure out where the snake could have gone. "Let's see now, the tank is near the piano—right on the piano bench."

"Look under the piano, Candoo," said Ms. Carrigan. Candoo got down on his hands and knees. He squinted as he tried to see if there was anything under the piano. He saw a little dust, but there was no snake.

"If the snake isn't *under* the piano," said Willdoo, "why don't we try to look *inside* the piano!" Ms. Carrigan opened the lid on the piano and peered inside. Sure enough, there was the boa constrictor, curled up contentedly way down at the bottom.

Ms. Carrigan reached inside the piano to lift the snake out, but her arm wasn't long enough! She could not reach the snake!

"How can we get the snake out of the piano?" someone asked.

Ms. Carrigan said, "Let's all think very hard and see how many ideas we can come up with to get the snake to come out of the piano."

Some of the children closed their eyes to help them think. Some looked around the room, hoping to get an idea from something they saw.

When Juan looked at the record player, he remembered something. "Ms. Carrigan," he said, "once I saw a picture of a man playing some music for a snake. The snake was coming out of a basket in front of the man. Maybe if we play a record, the snake will come out of the piano."

All of the children thought that was a good idea, so they decided to try it. They played a record, but there was no sign of the snake. She did not budge.

"Let's poke her with a yardstick," Khanh said. "She'll surely come out then!"

"Oh, no!" Willdoo cried. "We can't do that! We might hurt the snake, and we wouldn't want to do that! We'd better not try that idea!"

"I wonder if she likes candy," George said. "If she does, she might come out if we offered her some."

Ms. Carrigan had some candy in her desk. She tied some to a string and lowered it into the piano. But still the snake did not move.

"Well, we've tried two ideas now," Ms. Carrigan said. "We have to try all kinds of ideas even if some of them don't work. Let's keep thinking till we find one that does."

The children were quiet again as they tried hard to think of some more ideas. But each idea they tried didn't work. The snake stayed in the piano! Still, whenever one idea didn't work, the children would think of something else.

Finally, José said he had another idea for them to try. "We played nice soft music on the record player, and the snake didn't move. Maybe we should try something that is loud. She might not like noise. I will try making a lot of noise on the piano. If she doesn't like it, maybe she'll come out!"

The children held their hands over their ears. They didn't know how the snake felt, but they didn't like the noise at all! José banged the keys in the middle of the keyboard as hard as he could. Then he played the low notes—fast and hard.

Ms. Carrigan looked into the piano. "It's working, José!" she exclaimed. "She's starting to crawl out. Keep it up!"

José kept pounding on the piano as the children watched. "There she is!" they shouted, as the snake's head appeared over the top of the piano. Ms. Carrigan quickly picked up the snake and put her into the glass tank. This time Ms. Carrigan was very careful to fasten the lid tightly.

"Well," she said with a sigh of relief, "I'm glad that's over! I'd like to thank all of you for being so helpful. You certainly came up with a lot of ideas for getting the snake to come out!"

"But our ideas didn't all work," said Maria.

"That's true, Maria," Candoo said. "But we all helped out with ideas until we got one that did work, and that's all that matters!"

# Grandma's Sad Day

Willdoo and Candoo felt happy and excited because of their good day at school. When they got home from school, they rushed right up to their grandmother's room to tell her all about the things that had happened that day.

But Grandma did not seem interested in the things they were saying. She sat quietly as they talked, rocking slowly back and forth in her chair, hardly answering them. She seemed to be feeling sad.

Candoo and Willdoo went to ask their mother what was wrong. She explained that one of Grandma's best friends—someone she had known for many years—had died the day before. Grandma was missing her friend and feeling very sad.

Willdoo and Candoo felt sad too when they thought about how much their grandmother missed her friend. They wished she didn't feel so sad, and they wanted to help her.

"I think I know how Grandma feels," Willdoo said. "When I'm sad, I don't like to be alone. Maybe Grandma doesn't want to be alone either."

Willdoo and Candoo went back to Grandma's room and sat down by her chair. Candoo held Grandma's hand. Grandma said it helped her to have them with her when she was feeling sad. They all sat quietly for a while.

Then Grandma said, "I think I would like to go for a walk. Would you children like to go with me?" Willdoo and Candoo nodded eagerly, happy that their grandmother seemed to be feeling a little better.

It was a beautiful, warm day, and the children and their grandmother walked through the park near their house. When they got home, Candoo and Willdoo's mother had cookies and milk ready for them.

As they sat at the table eating, Grandma looked at Candoo and Willdoo and smiled. "I'm glad I have two grandchildren to keep me company when I'm sad," she said.

# The Play

Willdoo ran into the yard where a group of her friends were playing.

"I have a great idea!" she said. "Let's put on a play the way we do in school sometimes."

"That sounds like a good idea," Bonnie said. "I think the story of the Little Red Hen would make a good play. Let's do that one."

"Oh, no," Willdoo replied. "I've already picked out the story for our play. It's the one about the Three Billy Goats Gruff!"

Bonnie felt a little disappointed that Willdoo hadn't even listened to her idea, but Willdoo didn't seem to notice.

"Now let's see," Willdoo said. "First we'll need a bridge."

"I can make a good bridge," Gerry said eagerly. "I'll get a board and some boxes from the garage."

But before Gerry could move toward the garage, he heard Willdoo say, "No, Gerry, don't bother. I've already decided what we should use. You just wait here a minute, and I'll get it."

Gerry was disappointed that Willdoo wasn't interested in his idea, but Willdoo was so busy dragging the picnic bench across the yard that she didn't notice how Gerry felt.

"Now," said Willdoo, "we have to decide where to put the bridge."

"There's a little ditch by my house," said Juan. "That would be a good place. There isn't much water in it, so my mom won't get mad if we play there."

"No," said Willdoo, shaking her head. "We'll put it across that little path over there. We can pretend that the path is a river."

Juan felt annoyed. He thought using the ditch was a good idea, but Willdoo had completely ignored him!

Candoo and Gerry started walking over to pick up the bench, but they were too late. Willdoo was already pulling it across the yard to the path.

"There!" she said. "That's just right. That's just where I want it!"

"We need horns for the billy goats," Barry said. "I have a football helmet with horns on the sides at home. That would work for one billy goat."

But Willdoo said, "That won't work at all. I've got just the thing in the house. Stay here. I'll be back in a minute."

After a while Willdoo came out with some headbands and some feathers. She had put on a headband and tucked a feather in each side. "See," she said, "they look like horns."

Barry felt angry. He thought his football helmet would have worked just as well as Willdoo's feathers—maybe even better—but Willdoo hadn't paid any attention to his idea. Barry didn't like being ignored either.

Candoo had an idea. "I have a really scary monster mask I used on Halloween," he said. "The troll could wear my mask. It would be perfect!"

But Willdoo said, "No, I think I'll make something." And she ran into the house again.

Candoo was disappointed. He thought his mask would have been perfect for the troll, but Willdoo hadn't even listened to him.

After a while Willdoo came back with a paper bag. She had cut out holes for the eyes and had drawn a scary mouth on it with her crayons. She put it over her head. "There!" she giggled. "Don't I look just like an old troll?" No one answered her. Willdoo took off her mask, saying, "Now we have everything we need. We can have our——" And then she stopped. She looked around. No one was left in the yard except Candoo and Juan, and they were leaving!

"Where are you going?" Willdoo called out. "Where is everyone? I'm ready to have our play. I'm going to be the troll!"

"We're all going home," Juan told her.

And Candoo said, "I'm going over to Juan's. We're going to play with his trucks."

"But, wait a minute," Willdoo said. "What about the play? I have everything ready!" The children kept on walking while Willdoo stood there watching them.

"The play sure sounded like a good idea," she said to herself. "I wonder why they all went home."

# Please Play with Me

It was Saturday morning. Lena's mother was working on the car, and Lena was sitting on the front steps, watching her.

"I wish it wasn't Saturday," Lena said gloomily.

"What's wrong with Saturday?" her mother asked.

"There's no school on Saturday," said Lena, "so there's nobody to play with."

"Many of your school friends live close by," said Lena's mother. "Why don't you take a walk and see if you can find someone to play with?"

Lena sat quietly for a few minutes thinking about her mother's suggestion. "Oh, well," she said to herself, "I guess I'll give it a try. It will be better than being home alone all day."

Lena started down the street. As she walked by Juan's house, she saw Candoo and Juan in the backyard. They were playing with their trucks.

Lena went over to them. "Hi!" she said. "My mother said I should play with someone, and I'm going to play with you. You better let me play, or I'll tell my mother! Give me a truck!"

"Lena, you sure are being bossy," Juan said. "If you're going to be bossy, we don't want to play with you."

Lena turned around and ran all the way home. Her mother was still outside working on the car.

"I wanted to play with Candoo and Juan," Lena said to her mother, "but they wouldn't let me. Juan said I was too bossy." Looking very unhappy, Lena sat down on the steps.

"Why did Juan say you were bossy?" Lena's mother asked.

"Because I told them they had to give me a truck to play with. And because I said that I'd tell *you* if they didn't let me play!" said Lena.

"I'm afraid that Candoo and Juan were right, Lena. That was being bossy, and no one likes to be bossed around," said Lena's mother. "It's no fun if one person is always telling the others what to do."

Lena thought about what her mother had said. "Maybe I have been a little bossy," she thought to herself. "I will try to be kinder." She went into the house to get something and put it in her pocket. Then she started down the street again.

When Lena passed the vacant lot, she saw Willdoo and Barry pounding nails into some boards.

"Hi, Lena!" called Barry. "We're building a house."

"Can I play with you?" asked Lena.

"Sure," said Willdoo. "But we only have two hammers. You'll have to take turns."

But Lena didn't want to take turns. She wanted a hammer all to herself. She reached into her pocket and pulled out a piece of candy. "If you'll give me your hammer, Willdoo, I'll give you this candy," she said.

"No, Lena," said Willdoo. "I like to pound better than I like candy, and I want a turn."

Lena turned to Barry. "Barry, will *you* trade *your* hammer for some candy?" she asked.

"No," said Barry. "I like to pound too. Anyway, Lena, I'm not supposed to eat candy before lunch."

"Oh, who wants to hammer anyway!" Lena said angrily. She marched off down the street, saying, "I'll eat my candy by myself!"

When Lena got home, she told her mother what had happened. "Willdoo and Barry wouldn't play with me either. And I didn't boss them. I was very nice to them! I even told them I would give them candy."

"You don't have to give your friends candy," Lena's mother said, "to get them to play with you. If you're pleasant and friendly, and try to share, they'll want to play with you."

Lena went over to the steps and sat down again. She thought about what had happened that morning and about what her mother had said. After a while, she picked up her big green ball and held it on her lap.

"I like to play with my big ball by myself sometimes," she thought, "but right now I feel like playing ball *with* someone. Maybe if I share my ball, someone will play with me."

Just then Lena saw Aaron in his backyard. He was trying to fly a little glider plane.

Lena jumped up, holding her ball. "Aaron," she called, "do you want to play with me? We can play catch with my ball."

Aaron couldn't help noticing Lena's friendly smile as he looked over at her. He thought he would enjoy playing ball with her. "Just a minute," Aaron called back. "I'll tell my mother I'm coming over."

Soon Aaron came running across the backyard. "I'm glad you want to share your ball with me," he said. "Bounce it to me, Lena!"

Lena laughed and bounced her ball to Aaron. At last she'd found a good way to get someone to play with her!

# Grabby Grundel

One day, when Aaron and Lena were playing in Aaron's backyard, a boy walked by carrying a brown bag. He watched for a while as Aaron and Lena galloped around on their broomstick horses.

When Aaron noticed the boy, he called out, "Hello. What's your name?"

"I'm Grabby. Grabby Grundel," the little boy answered.

"Grabby Grundel!" said Lena. "That's a funny name. Is it *really* your name?"

"No, not my *real* name," said the boy. "But that's what everyone calls me."

Lena said, "Well, my name is Lena. And this is Aaron." She pointed to Aaron and then asked, "Do you want to play with us?"

Grabby Grundel said he would like to play, and they had a good time for a while, taking turns riding the two broomstick horses.

Then Grabby saw something. It was a paddle with a rubber string attached to it. On the other end of the string was a small rubber ball.

Grabby picked it up, looked at it, and then asked, "How does this thing work?"

"Oh, that's a paddle ball," Aaron said. "See, you hit the ball with the paddle. Then this string pulls the ball right back so that you can hit it again."

Grabby Grundel liked the paddle ball. Lena and Aaron went on playing with the broomstick horses, but Grabby played with the paddle ball.

When Aaron and Lena tired of riding and stopped their game, they realized that Grabby Grundel had left. Aaron looked around for his paddle ball, but he couldn't find it. He looked under the bushes and in the grass. He looked everywhere, but his paddle ball had disappeared. Aaron felt very gloomy. The paddle ball was one of his favorite toys, and he didn't like losing it. He sat down on the porch and frowned.

A few days later, Grabby Grundel went to Candoo and Willdoo's house. Some of the children were playing tag when Grabby Grundel walked into the yard carrying his brown bag. The children asked Grabby to play with them.

Grabby played with the children for a while, and then, when he sat down to rest, he saw something he liked. It was a can opener that belonged to Candoo.

"What's this?" asked Grabby as he picked up the can opener.

"That's my can opener," said Candoo, proudly. "I've always liked to play with it, so my mom gave it to me for my own."

Candoo showed Grabby how the can opener worked and how the gears moved when the handle was turned. While the rest of the children played tag, Grabby Grundel played with the can opener.

When the game was over, Grabby Grundel was gone . . . and so was Candoo's can opener. Candoo looked all over for it, but he couldn't find it anywhere. Candoo felt miserable.

A few days later, Grabby Grundel appeared with his brown bag in his hand at the playground where Rachel and her brother were playing on the swings.

Grabby sat down on one of the swings too. Then he noticed something on the ground. It was lying right next to Rachel's sweater. He reached over and picked it up. "What's this?" he asked Rachel.

"That's my bubble blower," Rachel told him. She showed Grabby how the shiny bubbles would flow out when the bubble blower was dipped in soapy water. Grabby kept looking at the bubble blower while Rachel and her brother were swinging.

When they had finished swinging, Grabby Grundel was gone. Rachel picked up her sweater and looked for her bubble blower. She looked all around, but her bubble blower was nowhere to be found. Rachel felt very unhappy as she walked slowly home.

The next day, Grabby, holding his brown bag, stopped at the vacant lot where the children were building their playhouse. For a while Grabby worked on the playhouse with the others. But then he saw Khanh's yo-yo lying on a tree stump.

Grabby picked it up. "What's this?" he asked.

"That's my yo-yo," said Khanh. "I'm pretty good at yo-yoing. Just watch me!"

Khanh showed Grabby how the yo-yo worked. Then he let Grabby try it out while he went back to work on the playhouse.

When the children were ready to go home, Grabby Grundel had left and Khanh could not find his yo-yo. He looked all over the lot, but the yo-yo was gone.

Khanh felt so upset that he sat down on the tree stump and cried.

Then one day, as the children were coming out of school, there was Grabby Grundel waiting for them. He had a lot of envelopes in his big brown bag. They were invitations for the children to come to Grabby's house for his birthday party.

When the day of the party came, all of the children gathered at Grabby's house. There was ice cream and cake for everyone, and the children played games.

But when the children went to play with Grabby's toys, what a surprise they got!

Aaron said, "Hey! That's *my* paddle ball."

"And that's *my* can opener," cried Candoo.

"There's *my* bubble blower," squealed Rachel.

"And *my* yo-yo!" shouted Khanh.

All the children stared at Grabby Grundel.

"I wanted to play with them some more," said Grabby, "so I took them home with me."

"But all those toys belong to someone else," Willdoo said. "How would you feel if we took all your birthday presents home with us because we wanted to play with them?"

Grabby looked at all his new toys. "I wouldn't like that at all," said Grabby. "I would really feel unhappy."

Then the children told Grabby how they felt when their toys were missing.

"I guess I never thought about how you would feel," Grabby said. "I didn't mean to make anyone angry. I won't do it anymore. If I play with your toys, I will leave them there when I go home."

After that, when Grabby came to play, he didn't bring his brown bag with him.

And after a while they didn't call him Grabby anymore. They called him Gordon, which was his real name.

# I'm Glad I Did That

Candoo was lying in bed, thinking about his day at school. He didn't like what he remembered.

There was Gerry's crumpled picture . . . Willdoo's broken sand castle . . . Aaron left alone to put away the Tinkertoys he and Candoo had shared. Candoo had done all of those things and, worst of all, he had called Mark a baby when Mark had trouble buttoning his paint shirt.

Candoo had made a lot of people unhappy that day. As he thought about the way he had behaved, Candoo didn't feel so happy himself.

"I wish I had not done those things," thought Candoo.

But it was too late for wishing. He *had* done all of those things.

"Well, one thing's for sure," Candoo promised himself. "I'm never going to act like that again!"

The next day at school Candoo and some of the other children were getting ready to finger paint. Candoo was in a hurry to begin. He put on his paint shirt and picked up his paper. But as he started for the table, he noticed Mark looking for someone to button his shirt.

Candoo opened his mouth to say, "Mark is a baby!" But then he remembered his promise to himself. "Would you like me to help you button your shirt, Mark?" Candoo asked.

Mark looked a little surprised, but he nodded and turned around so that Candoo could fasten the button in back.

"It's hard to button things in back, 'cause you can't see what you're doing," said Candoo. He hoped that Mark wouldn't feel bad because he needed help with the button.

After Candoo had fastened the shirt, Mark thanked him. Mark looked so pleased that Candoo thought to himself, "I'm glad I did that!"

Candoo went over to the table and started painting his picture. Gerry was already painting, and he was telling about his picture as he worked.

"See, this is my sailboat," said Gerry. "And there are big waves all around. And this is a cloud."

Candoo looked at the picture. He thought about making a big wind that would blow Gerry's boat over. He could make Gerry's boat go away by rubbing it off with his hand.

He reached over toward the picture, saying, "I have an idea——" But then, Candoo remembered. He put his hand back on his own paper and said, "Uh . . . I'll make a sailboat too, just like yours, Gerry. You and I are going to be on it—we'll be the sailors."

Gerry smiled at Candoo. "That sounds like a good idea, Candoo," he said happily.

And Candoo thought to himself, "I'm glad I did that!"

Ms. Carrigan played the piano. That meant it was cleanup time. Candoo finished wiping off the table where he had been working and hurried to put away his paint shirt. He wanted to be first in line to wash his hands for snack time.

He was ready to get in line when he saw Aaron. Aaron had made a make-believe birthday cake on the pegboard. It would take Aaron quite a while to put away all those pegs by himself. Candoo started to say, "I'm going to be first——" But he remembered, and instead he said, "I'll help you put away those pegs, Aaron. Then you won't have to be last in line."

Surprised, Aaron looked at Candoo. When he saw that Candoo really meant it, he grinned and said, "Thank you, Candoo. I could sure use some help."

Together, the two boys were able to put away all of the pegs quickly. Then they found places in the line.

And Candoo thought to himself, "I'm glad I did that!"

After school, Candoo found Willdoo playing in the sand behind the house. Willdoo had the handle of a wagon raised up high, with a sand pail hanging on the end of it.

"What are you doing, Willdoo?" Candoo asked curiously.

"I made a steam shovel," said Willdoo proudly, "just like Mike Mulligan's in the storybook at school."

Candoo looked at the steam shovel and realized it was his wagon Willdoo was using. He started to say, "Hey, that's my wagon——" But then he remembered. "Hey!" he said, "I never thought of making a steam shovel with the wagon. That's a good idea, Willdoo! Can I play with you?"

"That'll be fun!" said Willdoo. She felt pleased that Candoo liked her steam shovel.

As they began playing, Candoo thought to himself, "I'm glad I did that!"

That night when Candoo was lying in bed, he thought about his day, and he liked what he remembered.

# Different Groups

One Saturday morning, Willdoo and her dad were working in the garage. They were building a birdhouse to put up in their yard, and they were enjoying themselves as they worked together. Willdoo pounded the nails, and her dad did all the cutting with the electric saw. Willdoo was going to paint the house when it was finished. Building was one of the things Willdoo liked to do most of all.

While they were working, a car drove into their driveway. Nancy and Gwen jumped out of the car and ran up to Willdoo.

"Do you want to go swimming with us?" Gwen asked. "Our mother is taking a group of us to the pool today."

Another time Willdoo would have enjoyed going swimming with the group, but today she said, "No, thank you. I'm building a birdhouse with my dad."

"Okay, we'll ask you another time," Nancy said, and the girls got back into the car.

Willdoo and her dad had just started to work again
when another group of children came up their driveway.

"Hey, Willdoo!" Greg called. "Come and play kickball
with us."

"Thanks for asking me," Willdoo replied, "but I'm busy
now. I'm building a birdhouse with my dad."

"Okay," said Greg. "If you want to play later, come on
down to my house." And Greg and the rest of the group
went to play ball.

A little while later, Barry rode up on his bicycle.

"Hi, Willdoo. What are you building?" he asked.

"My dad and I are making a birdhouse," Willdoo answered.

"That looks like it's going to be a great birdhouse," Barry said.

Willdoo thought Barry might like to build too, so she said, "You can help us if you want to."

Barry eagerly accepted Willdoo's invitation. He was excited about helping to build the birdhouse. He liked to pound the nails too. The three of them worked together to build a good birdhouse.

After a while, Willdoo's dad said, "You know, we could call this the birdhouse-building group. We are all working on the birdhouse, and we are a group."

"That's right," said Willdoo. "There were three groups here today. There was the first group, the swimming group: all of them were going to go swimming. And there was the second group, the kickball group: all of them were going to play kickball."

Barry laughed and said, "And we are group number three. We're the birdhouse-building group."

The birdhouse-building group had a good day together. They worked hard, and when they were all finished, they had built a sturdy new home for some lucky bird family.